Our Foreign Travel Diary

BIKRAM BANERJEA
AJITA BANERJEA

BLUEROSE PUBLISHERS
India | U.K.

Copyright © Bikram Banerjea and Ajita Banerjea 2024

All rights reserved by author. No part of this publication may be reproduced, stored in a retrieval system or transmitted in any form or by any means, electronic, mechanical, photocopying, recording or otherwise, without the prior permission of the author. Although every precaution has been taken to verify the accuracy of the information contained herein, the publisher assume no responsibility for any errors or omissions. No liability is assumed for damages that may result from the use of information contained within.

BlueRose Publishers takes no responsibility for any damages, losses, or liabilities that may arise from the use or misuse of the information, products, or services provided in this publication.

For permissions requests or inquiries regarding this publication, please contact:

BLUEROSE PUBLISHERS
www.BlueRoseONE.com
info@bluerosepublishers.com
+91 8882 898 898
+4407342408967

ISBN: 978-93-5819-716-7

Cover design: Tahira
Typesetting: Tanya Raj Upadhyay

First Edition: February 2024

FOREWORD

SRI SRI MA ANANDAMAYEE SMARANAM

This book on our TRAVELOGUE covers from 1979 onwards with the middle east in Baghdad, the Iraqi capital & wrapping up in Portugal during 2023 summer. Some of the articles appeared after our travel to different countries in Times of India, supplements published in Mumbai. Due to requests received from our friends in Mumbai & other travel companions from other countries we took to this endeavor. Before we conclude if we did not mention our elder grandson Arnab Chaudhuri's name, then this will be highly unjustified, as he was instrumental in getting this book published especially by Bluerose Publishers, so we express our gratitude to them for taking up this venture.

TABLE OF CONTENTS

BEGUILING VISIT TO DRESDEN 1

BOWLED OVER BY BERLIN 7

THE HILLS ARE ALIVE-SALZBURG 11

ENTHRALLING VISIT TO ROYAL CITY VIENNA (WIEN) 13

ENCHANTING PRAGUE VISIT 16

ROMAN HOLIDAY 20

BONJOUR PARIS 26

HELLO (HOLA) SPAIN 35

AMAZING VISIT TO LIECHTENSTEIN AND SWITZERLAND 41

SPARKLING SOUTH KOREA 45

MEMORIES OF THE MIDDLE EAST 49

    SEPTEMBER THE 11TH, 2001 - THE MIDDLE EAST PRE-9/11: 49

    MEMORIES OF IRAQ: 50

    MEMORIES OF IRAN: (1985- '87) 51

ENCHANTING SLOVENIA CROATIA AND BOSNIA 56

    TRIP PLANNING 56

    SLOVENIA 57

CROATIA	59
SPLIT	61
ISTANBUL	67
A VISIT TO NIAGARA FALLS	75
BRANDENBERG ROYALS-THE CRYPT	77
BEGUILING VOLLENDAM & AMSTERDAM	80
OUR LONDON VISIT	83
OUR US SOJOURN IN 2009	86
A DAY IN BRUSSELS	91
ENCHANTING PORTUGAL SOJOURN	93
ALFAMA	94
RESTORADOUR (RESTORER)	95
PALACE	96
MIRADOURO SANTA LUZIA	96
BELEM TOWER (TORRE DE BELEM)	97
PORTO	98
THE ALGARVE	102

BEGUILING VISIT TO DRESDEN

During our second visit to this East German city in May 2011, we were spellbound by the intrinsic natural beauty of this small city. It is located 205 km south of Berlin, the capital of the German Democratic Republic (GDR). It was indeed a memorable tour, thanks to its soothing natural beauty. In Eastern Europe, this city stands out with extraordinary Baroque architectural edifices, along with the meandering River Elbe flowing along the shoreline. The city bears the testimony of the Second World War, as evident in the blackened war-damaged facades of buildings, palaces, and more. These structures, among others, are being restored with appropriate materials and expertise to retain their original features. Notably, many visitors tour this city from the neighborhood, with few encounters with Indians but a significant presence of Japanese and Koreans from the Asian continent.

The locals call Dresden "Dresn." This city is often compared to Florence, the popular Italian tourist destination, earning the nickname "Elbeflorenz." The ochre and green-shaded buildings and structures bear witness to the war-damaged portions duly blackened.

This city, in terms of area, is the same as Berlin, but back then, the population was only half a million compared to Berlin's three million. At that time,

Mumbai's population was 14 million. Due to the meager population in the city, we hardly encountered anyone when we lost our way.

In 1945, continuous bombing during February 13-15 caused the city to burn for days. Even after nearly seven decades, most of the churches and castles (Schlosses) still bear the testimony to the damages caused by the war. The top regions of the churches and buildings still bear these black marks.

As mentioned before, this city was the capital of the Saxony in the 15th century. Although most of the edifices boasting the best architectural creations were built in the 18th century by Royal Augustus the Strong. A bridge over the Elbe River was named after him during the reign of Frederick the Second Augustus, his son. Many places in the city gave the impression that the revival was far from completion.

We stayed on Dr. Kulz Ring Street in a famous US hotel chain in front of an old traditional store, Karstadt. This store was built in 1915, but back then, it was not completed in all respects. On the southern side of the Elbe river shore, on the extreme south street, a viewing gallery at a higher level was there, offering an excellent view of the Elbe river and the horizon of Dresden during the sunset at 9 pm in May. The silhouette of the city at this hour was an unforgettable sight. This viewing balcony is known as the Gallery of Europe, where tourists would gather in the evening to enjoy the sight, the music played by buskers, and local food. We particularly enjoyed the "Mama Mia" songs performed by the buskers.

Some of the must-visit places in Dresden are enumerated as follows:

i) Zwinger Palace & Museum. ii) Katholische Hopkirsche (Catholic Church). iii) Hygiene Museum. iv) Zoo (extraordinarily curated with a variety of exotic animal stock). v) Semperperer (The Concert Theatre). vi) Freunkirsche (Our Lady Church). vii) Numismatics (300,000 coins, medieval period banknotes, and many exotic artifacts). viii) Grunes Gewolbe (Green Vault) - Notable for the 1707-08 period sculpture depicting Mughal King Aurangjeb's court scene in gold by an Italian goldsmith named Dinglinger. The best creations of Dinglinger, such as the hat hanger made of green diamonds and 185 pieces of different facial expressions made from cherry-shaped rubies, are remarkable. Silverwork with engraved precious stones is also featured.

On the way to Zwinger Palace, porcelain tiles on the walls with mural work of the Saxonies over the centuries attract tourists from all over the world.

Most of the churches in the city arrange concerts. One Friday, we attended such a concert, buying tickets for Euro 17. The concert was presented by the world-famous Maestro Kurt Masur, who had conducted the New York Philharmonic and the Israeli Philharmonic, among many others. The concert was so exceptional that the audience gave a standing ovation that night. It was our first opportunity to listen to such a grand concert.

Briefly, we made a visit to Meissen through a short Elbe river cruise and later to Pilnitz. Meissen was the place where porcelain was first created in Europe, and we saw amazing porcelain artifacts crafted by the artisans. Thus, the enriching visit to Dresden folded up, but the memories are still vivid in our minds.

BOWLED OVER BY BERLIN

When you think of Berlin, the name Adolf Hitler often comes to mind. However, the most surprising thing we discovered was that the local Berliners and Germans, in general, were soft-spoken and sober, showing no signs of a Nazi leader.

This city is famous, especially for the World War II events that took place, which are unforgettable. Berlin is also renowned for the Berlin Wall, a part of which was still standing for tourists to see. Berlin is located on the banks of the Spree River. We visited the place where the construction of this wall began. This wall divided the state into two parts, and besides the Berlin Wall, we also visited the Brandenburg Gate, which attracts tourists due to its historical significance as a monument that once divided Germany into two. This place witnessed restrictions on the movement of East and West Germans.

The Brandenburg Gate is a famous edifice that showcases German architectural excellence. After the Berlin Wall was demolished, this historic gate became a symbol of German reunification. It was originally built in 1719 by Frederick Wilhelm as a memorial for undivided Berlin. When Berlin was split into two, our guide explained in detail the difficulties that Germans faced in their daily lives. On the day of our visit, a demonstration was taking place, with protestors demanding the conservation of nature and the preservation of ecological balance. These demonstrators represented a group called GREEN EARTH.

We also explored Charlottenburg Palace, one of the largest palaces in Europe. Frederick the Great expanded the palace between 1740 and 1742. The palace's interior was enchanting and well-preserved, surrounded by Baroque-style gardens that transformed it into a beautiful landscape. Originally built as a summer residence for Prussian Queen Sophie Charlotte, subsequent rulers extended it. It holds a significant place in the history of architectural accomplishments and is a must-see for tourists.

Our visit to the Bode Museum on the banks of the Spree River was also memorable. The museum, built by Wilhelm von Bode, features artifacts crafted between the 17th and 18th centuries, including exquisite ivory and woodwork. These pieces were skillfully handcrafted by artists like Leonherd Kem, Joachim Henn, and Adam Lenckhardt. Johan Danielle Sommer crafted a spellbinding armoire in 1685 using the Boulle method, which resembles the outer shell of a tortoise covered by a metallic overlay.

Berlin Zoo, established in 1844, is one of the oldest zoos on the planet. This zoo was a gift from Prussian King Friedrich Wilhelm IV to the city of Berlin. The famous Alexander Von Humboldt, Martin Hinrich

Lichtenstein, and the renowned landscape artist and architect Peter Joseph Lenne were all involved in its establishment, with Peter Joseph Lenne's creations in the zoo complex testifying to his brilliant work.

During our stay in Berlin, we chose the centrally located Stiglitz International Hotel. The city was always vibrant, with tourists, mostly from other parts of Europe, seen walking around and enjoying the city's features. Many shops and roadside stalls attracted crowds of tourists.

There was a square (locally known as "platz"). Every Thursday, a flea market was held here, where people from various backgrounds, including Vietnamese, Filipinos, Pakistanis, Ceylonese, Chinese, Indians, and other immigrants, traded reasonably priced items. The market was lively, with tourists often bargaining for the items they wished to purchase. Haggling was a common practice. In 2014, traveling by public transport and the metro was reasonably economical and comfortable.

As a teacher, my wife, Ajita, and I had the opportunity to meet some local school students while visiting the Brandenburg Gate. We engaged in conversations with them and learned about the German school education system. Education was conducted in three stages: up to the twelfth standard in Gymnasium, which included foreign language instruction. Middle school covered up to the tenth standard, with foreign languages introduced from the ninth standard onwards. These students were curious about India, and we exchanged currency coins and addresses.

When visiting Berlin or any place in Germany, it's important to be aware that pointing fingers is considered threatening. Indian cuisine is very popular in this country and is often more affordable than local German food. Berlin is home to many Turkish immigrants, and their roadside food stalls, selling kebabs, were always bustling. The kebabs were so large that it could be quite challenging to eat them without spilling.

Tourists were shown the two-room apartment of the German Chancellor, Angela Merkel, where she used to reside. It was appreciated to see how simply the head of the country lived.

Our trip to Germany concluded with the intention of visiting this beautiful European capital again.

THE HILLS ARE ALIVE-SALZBURG

At the end of May 2007, we embarked on an overland journey from Prague, the capital of the Czech Republic, to Salzburg. In this stunningly beautiful and compact city, the legendary Western Classical Music composer Wolfgang Amadeus Mozart once lived. The world-famous musical film "THE SOUND OF MUSIC" was shot on location in this city. Salzburg, known for its divine scenic beauty, is divided by the Salzac River, flowing from the northwest to the southeast.

Salzburg is a focal point for all Western classical music lovers. During July and August, a massive music festival is held here, attracting world-famous musicians and music connoisseurs. In the local language, these music programs are called "Konzerts." To attend this musical soirée, one needs to book accommodation in advance, as hotels fill up quickly. During our visit, we had the opportunity to go to the Concert Hall, where we were amazed by its gigantic auditorium, capable of holding 11,000 people. The stage was also large enough to accommodate 500 musicians with their instruments.

The city's name has an intriguing origin. In the medieval period, a salt mine was discovered here, and the word "Salz" (meaning salt) was incorporated into the city's name. In 696 AD, Bishop Rupert received this place as a gift from the Bavarian Duke Theodore. The city used to generate significant revenue from salt taxes.

While strolling through the city center, we visited the birthplace of the world-famous musician Mozart, which was a thrilling experience. The murals adorning the ceiling dome of the Cathedral left us enthralled. We explored the charming alleys, encountering many boutiques and eateries. The famous 1964 Hollywood musical, shot in Salzburg, made this city a renowned tourist destination. Our guide took us to the locations where the film was shot, including Mirabell Gardens and the Cathedral, from where Captain Von Trapp and his family fled.

We ascended to Hohen Salzburg by funicular and marveled at the castle perched on the hill. The castle was a treasure trove of wonders, and we enjoyed a bird's-eye view from the top, gazing at the meandering Salzac River and the town below, which looked breathtaking.

Our three-day stay in Salzburg was regrettably short. Nevertheless, we still harbor the hope of making another visit to this unforgettable tiny town.

ENTHRALLING VISIT TO ROYAL CITY VIENNA (WIEN)

While traveling through historically significant Eastern Europe, we eventually arrived in the Austrian capital, Vienna. This stunningly beautiful city is on the banks of the Danube River. Vienna is home to two world-famous celebrities: Sigmund Freud, the psychologist, and Ludwig von Beethoven, the Western classical music composer, who both resided here.

Another Western classical music genius, Mozart, lived in Vienna and created incredible symphonies during his time in the city. Mozart also passed away in Vienna. Many great musicians visited Vienna, and their recorded performances are carefully preserved in museums located in the Museum Quarter, known locally as MQ. We were so excited to explore the unique features of this city that we decided to venture out on our own, clutching a route map to navigate the city. However, our adventure didn't go as planned, and we got lost. Thanks to the friendly approach of the locals, they guided us safely back to our hotel.

We took the metro from a station close to our hotel and got off at MQ to visit the museums. First, we visited the Leopold Museum, where we witnessed many modern artifacts. Then, we explored the Kinder Museum (Children's Museum), where kids showcased offset printing, shared insights on carbon footprints, and demonstrated how to create useful domestic essentials from paper rejects. Ajita interacted with an African female supervisor who was guiding the children in making these items.

Afterward, we strolled through the glittering shopping area along Mariahilfer Strausse. We noticed that, in addition to European tourists, there were many visitors from Southeast Asia. We observed that Indian ladies wearing sarees caught the attention of both the locals and other tourists.

Following this, we visited St. Stephen's Church, a 600-year-old cathedral that reminded us of the Cologne Cathedral in Germany, especially considering the design of the dome and the entrance facade.

The next day, we visited Schönbrunne Palace. This potentially majestic edifice is located in a vast area, featuring a beautifully laid-out garden that transports visitors to the incredible world of the Baroque architectural period. Upon entering the palace, we discovered a wealth of information about the royals, which was quite intriguing. The palace itself boasts of a staggering 1400 rooms, but only 40 of them are open to tourists. Schönbrunne was named after a spring that has been forgotten for many years. In 1695, Johan Bernard Fisur instructed his architect to construct a residence using the Baroque architectural style. In the 18th century, Empress Maria Theresia completed the palace. She had 16 children, and it's worth noting that electricity for the palace was provided by none other than Thomas Edison himself. Currently, many European concerts are held in the palace forecourt, featuring world-famous maestros like André Rieu, the renowned Italian singer Andrea Bocelli, and others who perform live.

As we left the palace, the souvenir shop caught the attention of all tourists, including us. We purchased a CD titled "Wiener Waltz."

One of the most intriguing features in this palace was that every room was equipped with heating facilities, as the nights used to be chilly. Gold-plated wooden artifacts and brilliant paintings left tourists in awe. The garage was adorned with French woolens from Leon, France.

Though we didn't stay in Vienna for many days, we still vividly remember the places, the people, and the city itself.

ENCHANTING PRAGUE VISIT

In 2007, we visited the picturesque city of Prague, the capital of the Czech Republic, known locally as 'Praha.' It was during the summer when we explored this city, which is situated on the banks of the Vlatva River, flowing through Hungary and Germany. Our journey from Dresden to Prague via an overland bus was a captivating experience, with the natural surroundings on either side of the road, especially the meadows, being spellbinding. The meadows were adorned with wavering poppy flowers, enhancing the natural beauty and leaving us enthralled. As we neared Prague, the Czech capital, the natural beauty continued to unfold. We admired the red-tiled, sloping-roofed houses perched on the hills, which were simply breathtaking.

Our arrival in Prague brought us to the Crown Plaza Hotel in the town center. The hotel was quite large and was famous as the place where Hollywood stars, including Daniel Craig, stayed for a night during their journey to the shooting zone of the movie "Casino Royale." We learned this interesting tidbit from the hotel's concierge.

The next morning, accompanied by our Czech guide Maria, we embarked on a city tour. Our first destination was the world-renowned Prague Castle.

This vast castle, covering an area of 7 hectares, was built by Prince Borivoj of the Premislid Royal dynasty in 880 AD and is known as the largest castle on the planet. The first stone-walled structure within the castle is the Merry Mother's Church, which now serves as a museum showcasing multifaceted artifacts. In the 10th century AD, Prague Castle was used by the Czech Prince, then by the king, and later by Church clerics. A significant period in the history of Prague Castle occurred during the reign of Charles IV (1346-1378) when it was occupied by the Holy Roman Emperors. During this time, the Church underwent refurbishments, and its security was enhanced. The flawless and undivided ochre obelisk granite stone sculpture left us spellbound. The stone steps leading down to the castle's periphery were made of granite, and our guide showed the watermarks as testimony to the fearsome and destructive floods of 2002 when the river overflowed the city. Such devastating floods had not occurred in the last five centuries.

Following our visit to Prague Castle, we strolled across the famous Charles Bridge, spanning over the Vlatva River. This Gothic-style bridge connects the old city with Malestrana, the other part of the city. During its early centuries, the bridge was known as Kammeny Bridge.

The Roman King Charles IV, prior to constructing the bridge, consulted an astronomer. This astronomer advised him to start the bridge construction in the year

1357, as this year comprises all prime numbers. The person supervising this construction was the architect Petre Parler, who also built the St. Vitus Cathedral in Prague Palace. It is said that, to make the bridge sturdy and resilient, egg yolks were mixed into the mortar used for stone masonry. Possibly due to this, Charles Bridge still stands sturdy and solid, defying floods and natural calamities over time. The view from the bridge, especially the silhouette of the city's buildings at dusk, is unforgettable.

After visiting Charles Bridge, we made our way to Prague University campus and then reached the world-famous Astronomical Clock. A huge crowd of tourists from almost every part of the world had gathered there. Everyone waited eagerly to hear the chimes of the Astronomical Clock.

Next, we visited a Bohemian Crystal shop, where we saw some glittering and excellent works of art, reminiscent of Swarovski in Austria. While buying Bohemian Crystal as a souvenir, we had a conversation with a Bulgarian salesgirl, leading to an exchange of languages. In Bulgarian, "thanks" is "Blagedara." During 2007, we bought some Czech currency; at that time, 30 Czech Crowns were equivalent to 1 Euro.

There is a wooden doll/toy market where beautiful children's toys are crafted from wood. Marionettes, the wooden dolls, caught our attention. Local children were often seen playing with these wooden dolls, and there are special rooms for displaying the marionettes. Dramas are also held, with the two main characters being Spejbi and Hurvinek.

Most streets in Prague were packed with tourists. We visited the BATA shoe store, a seven-story building manned by seven girls only.

In Prague, while the locals may not always appear very friendly, our guide mentioned that despite political separation, there is no bad blood between the Czechs and the Slovaks.

And thus, our visit to Prague came to an end. Nevertheless, we fondly recall the memories of our time there.

ROMAN HOLIDAY

On August 12th, 2013, our Turkish airliner landed in Rome (Roma), the historic capital of Italy. We immediately felt the vibrant atmosphere of this world-famous Italian city, known for its rich history that has intrigued wanderers for centuries. Rome is essentially an open-air museum, and it is also home to Vatican City, the spiritual center for the world's 1.2 billion Roman Catholics.

During our week-long sojourn, we had the opportunity to explore some remarkable historic monuments that date back 2000 years. Our journey began at the Trevi Fountain (Fontana Di Trevi), a Baroque architectural marvel built by Clament the XIII during the reign of Nicholas Salvi in 1762. This fountain was designed in such a way that it entirely covers the front facade of the nearby palace. Roman tradition held that anyone who visited the fountain and threw a coin into it while facing away would have their wishes fulfilled and would return to Rome. In our case, we followed this tradition during our first visit, & yes we visited Rome once again .Nevertheless, we noticed that most tourists adhered to this custom, and it was clear that the Roman Municipality generated substantial revenue from the coins. I once read in "The Times" London that a municipal employee was caught stealing these coins and was penalized by the authorities.

Next, we visited a prehistoric monument that had been destroyed and later rebuilt by Hadrian. In the 7th century, it was converted into a church. We strolled from Piazza del Popolo to Piazza Novonna, a sprawling square lined with restaurants and street performers entertaining tourists with music and dance. This place is ideal for spending time with family. We also admired a golden-domed church in the vicinity.

On another day, we ventured to the world-famous pilgrimage site, Saint Peter's Basilica. In the 15th century BC, the capricious Roman King Nero killed Saint Peter and buried him here. A Christian king later built this pilgrimage site. The Sistine Chapel, adorned with the magnificent creations of renowned painter and artist Michelangelo, is a must-see within the basilica. Additionally, we visited the National Museum of Modern Art, where we admired works by world-renowned artists such as Corbett, Rodin, Boldeni, Cezzane, Degas, and Monet. Each piece of art was exceptional. On our way back, we revisited Piazza del Popolo, and once again, we were awestruck by the stunning beauty of the city.

After visiting Vatican City, our next stop was the Colosseum, a semi-circular Amphitheatre constructed in 80 AD. It is also known as the Flavian Amphitheatre, named after the Flavian dynasty's first emperor, who initiated its construction. The Colosseum is renowned for its three classic architectural styles: Doric, Ionic, and Corinthian. This open-air arena hosted various events during Roman rule, including deadly fights between gladiators and ferocious animals. Chariot races were among its most popular attractions. From the Colosseum, we proceeded to the Forum, where Italian archaeologists were actively restoring its existing features. Along the way, we encountered landmarks like the Constantine Monument, Imperial Forum, and creations by emperors Caesar, Augustus, Trojan, Nerva, and Vespasian.

During our stay in Rome, we lodged at Hotel Domus Pacis in Terra Rossa, conveniently located near the Vatican Enclave. Cornelia Metro station was within close proximity to our hotel, making it easy for us to explore the city. We often indulged in sweet watermelons sold by street vendors, frequently buying from a Pakistani vendor from Lahore for €2. In Italian, watermelons are called "Coco Meru."

On one occasion, we were invited for lunch by the Mother Superior of a church in Mumbai funded by the Vatican, where I had worked as a consulting engineer. While staying in Rome, we were offered accommodation within the Vatican Enclave. However, certain restrictions prevented us from accepting this offer. We had the opportunity to meet some sisters working in the Papal office, who shared how occupied they were with their office duties. Our Pauline Convent sisters from Mumbai arranged a special visit to the

Vatican during morning mass, which was a truly memorable experience. The queues to enter Vatican City are typically incredibly long, and the Swiss Guards stationed there all look so similar that they could have been cast from the same mould.

Let me now share our experience of visiting Naples (Napoli) and Capri. We embarked on an overland bus journey from Rome to Naples, with Mount Vesuvius, famous for its volcanic eruptions, visible along the way. From Naples, we took a catamaran cruise through the Tyrrhenian Sea to reach Capri. As we approached Capri, we marveled at the picturesque, terraced cottages dotting the limestone hills. Our guide informed us that some Hollywood celebrities owned cottages here, including George Clooney, Leonardo DiCaprio, and Al Pacino. We had a pre-arranged lunch in Capri, which featured items such as pizzas, Russian salad, and popular Italian red wine. The pizza we tasted in Capri was possibly the most delicious we had ever tasted.

Our next destination was back in Rome. During our stay at the hotel, we befriended a family from Kazakhstan who suggested that we should not leave Rome without visiting Zoo Marine, located a bit outside the city. Responding to their advice, we embarked on a journey to Zoo Marine by first taking the Metro from our usual station, Cornelia, to the terminus. From there, we boarded a bus bound for Zoo Marine, which took almost an hour to reach.

Upon arrival, we realized that visiting this place was an excellent decision as it offered a host of enjoyable attractions. However, the most unusual situation we encountered was that we were the only people fully clothed, as the local Romans were in swimwear, as it was essentially a water park. The most captivating show we witnessed at Zoo Marine was the Dolphin show, held in a pool surrounded by viewing galleries. Four Italian women in their swimsuits conducted the show, and the dolphins danced in the pool to rhythmic music, creating an unforgettable visual delight. The spectators applause added to the excitement. Following the Dolphin show, we enjoyed a Sea Lion show. This type of entertainment is popular among Romans during the summer. In 2013, when we visited the zoo, the entry fee was €25 per person.

The next day, we began our exploration from the Spanish Steps (Piazza di Spagna). This is one of the most significant tourist spots, and it was named after the Spanish acquisition of the area in the 17th century when the Royal Spanish Steps were constructed. It gained further fame in 1953 when the iconic Hollywood film "Roman Holiday," starring Gregory Peck and Audrey Hepburn, was filmed there. We climbed the steps to the top, where many renowned hotels and stone-walled residences were located. On the other side, there was a cobbled stone road.

The significant historic spots and the fond memories of our visit to Rome since 2013 still remain vivid in our minds.

BONJOUR PARIS

We arrived at Charles De Gaulle Airport in Paris at 9:30 am local time via a Swiss Airline flight from Zurich. This airport also had the unique feature of twin runways over the adjacent freeway, similar to Schiphol in Amsterdam.

Paris

Our European host, Mr. Yannick, arranged airport transport via a SUV to reach our hotel, Port de Montreuil (in French, Montoro). This hotel was located on the eastern fringe of the city, an area predominantly inhabited by Africans and scattered East Europeans. We observed that every Saturday, Sunday, and

Monday, a flea market was held, offering a wide range of products with sellers from North Africa, Spain, Italy, Ukraine, Turkey, Egypt, Lebanon, Pakistan, Iran, and more, most of whom were migrants. Prices were reasonable, but haggling was necessary. The items traded included wristwatches, dresses, imitation jewellery, electronic goods, carpets, and healthcare products. This market was always bustling with buyers, although no French citizens were seen there.

Our tour began with the Eiffel Tower (Tour de Eiffel, locally called). Seeing the long line of tourists reminded us of the queues at the Shirdi Saibaba temple in India. The tower's second story is located at the 43rd level, which we reached using an elevator, as climbing the 1700 steps was not feasible. The elevator accommodated 60 persons. The views of Paris city from the top of the tower were simply breathtaking, especially on either side of the Seine River, where the houses on the banks presented a spectacular sight.

Gustav Eiffel designed this tower in 1889, and it was constructed with 2.8 million rivets and 10,000 tons of steel. In 1909, there were plans to dismantle the tower, but it was repurposed for transmitting radio messages due to its altitude. Today, tourists from around the world visit this steel wonder.

<u>Eiffel Tower</u>

Our next stop was Musee de Louvre (pronounced as Luv). This world-famous museum displayed great works of art by Leonardo Da Vinci, Tintoretto, Van Gogh, and many other renowned artists. One would need at least a week to cover the 30,000 artifacts on display. We visited twice, once in 2005 and again in 2012, with an entry fee of 10 Euros, but it was free on the first Sunday of the month.

From the Louvre, we walked through Jardin du Tuileries, where locals were sunbathing in high temperatures. We then reached the Arc de Triomphe, built by Napolean I in 1805 as a symbol of victory. Next was the world-famous pedestrianized street, Champs de Elysees, lined with nightclubs like Moulin Rouge, Lido, famous automobile manufacturers' shops, McDonald's, and more.

We proceeded to Concord Square, named for its role as a peaceful gathering spot. Here, we observed a

23-meter-tall, 3300-year-old pink obelisk made from a single granite stone weighing 230 tons. King Louis XVI and 1343 others were decapitated at this site.

We also visited an office complex in Montparnasse, where the 59-floor building's terrace provided a panoramic 360-degree view of the city.

Our next stop was Musee du Orsay, a disused railway station transformed into a museum. It featured multiple-level galleries with works of art by famous European artists like Sezen, Van Gogh, Degus, Monet, and more.

A Seine River cruise is a must in Paris, and we took a catamaran from the foot of the Eiffel Tower, cruising through 22 bridges connecting the shores. The illuminated monuments, laser beams projected onto the Eiffel Tower, and famous landmarks were unforgettable.

<u>Versailles Palace</u>

We also visited the French Catholic Church, 'Butte de Montmartre,' located on a hilly area accessible by a funicular. At the top, we saw the 'Basilique du Sacre Coeur' (Sacred Heart Basilica), built in 1870-'71 to commemorate the war between France and Prussia. This memorial resembles Kolkata's Victoria Memorial. The construction began in 1873 but didn't earn religious sanctity until 1917. Visitors can climb 234 steps to get a view of the city skyline up to 30 km on a clear day. The nearby narrow alley, lined with curio shops and sketch artists drawing portraits, reminded us of Salzburg.

One more must-visit in Paris is Notre Dame Cathedral, one of the most beautiful examples of Gothic-style architecture. The construction of this cathedral began in 1163 and was completed in 1343. The church is 130 meters long, 48 meters wide, and 35 meters high, with seats for 6000 members. A few years ago, the cathedral suffered a severe fire, which temporarily prohibited entry. We also had the chance to observe a rare bird, the Kestrel, which attracts many bird enthusiasts to the area.

Afterward, we visited Versailles Palace, located 25 kilometers from Paris, another magnificent wonder. Thanks to our French hosts, Mr. and Mrs. Yannick, who drove us to Versailles, we had the opportunity to learn about French customs, traditions, and culture. On the way, we passed by the road leading to Roland Garros, where the French Open Tennis matches are held.

The sprawling Versailles Palace, built by King Louis XVI, known as the Sun King (Roi Soleil), required the labor of 30,000 workers and reportedly drained the royal treasury. The palace complex has four major sections. While the 580-meter-long palace with its countless rooms is gorgeously decorated, only a few sections are open to tourists. The vast meadows and musical fountains on the west side attracted many visitors. To cover all these areas, we had to take a Train bus due to time constraints.

We also visited the Technical Museum of Paris, where an audio-visual program was featured. A helicopter was on display, providing an idea of the museum's immense size.

Musee de Rodin is another must-visit destination in Paris, displaying the world-famous sculptures of the great sculptor Auguste Rodin. This residence of Rodin was gifted to the federal authority according to Rodin's specified condition. "The Thinker," one of the world's most renowned sculptures, is housed here, attracting tourists from around the world. However, during our 2012 visit, efforts were made to maintain this work of art as it was starting to deteriorate.

During our time in Paris, we had the pleasure of meeting our friend Sharmila Roy Pommot, who invited us to attend a function at the Indian Embassy, graced by the Indian Ambassador. Our French host, Mr. Yannick, also joined us. Sharmila Roy Pommot sang a Tagore song at the function, and an Indian author launched a book. The event concluded with Indian refreshments courtesy de the Ambassador.

During our tour of Paris, we noticed that traveling by rented cars or taxis was prohibitively expensive, so we chose to use the Metro, which was not only faster but also more cost-effective. We became accustomed to Metro travel, which allowed us to observe the Parisians, who appeared very attractive but generally not very friendly. We also encountered many North Africans, especially Algerians, Moroccans, and Tunisians. Most Metro entrances featured street musicians.

I would highly recommend using the Metro for those planning to visit Paris to save on travel expenses and time. The signages are easy to read and use, and it's advisable to obtain a Metro Railway route plan for convenient travel. We are grateful to our son-in-law, whose business colleague hosted us in his posh residence in an elite arrondissement near Louis Pasteur station. Our son-in-law gifted him a crate of Indian mangoes, which they greatly enjoyed. Unfortunately, Mr. Yannick's wife, who used to prepare Rabbit curry (a delicacy in France), passed away in 2019 due to cancer. In France, English is not a widely spoken language, so having some knowledge of French vocabulary is essential for conversation with the locals. In Paris, sixteen percent of the population consists of immigrants, primarily from North Africa, as mentioned earlier. Our memories of this wonderful city will be etched in our minds forever.

HELLO (HOLA) SPAIN

In June 2019, we embarked on a journey to Spain, having been invited by our friends, Mr. and Mrs. Sengupta. They had rented an apartment in a centrally located area of Madrid, which we shared. On June 2nd, we arrived in Madrid, one of the most beautiful tourist spots in Western Europe and the capital of Spain. Madrid greeted us with spotlessly clean streets adorned with large trees, creating perfect avenues. The city boasted of sprawling green parks spread throughout, and we were truly captivated by the lush greenery of this amazing Spanish capital. In 2019, Madrid had a population of six and a half lakh, ranking third after Berlin and Rome among European capitals. In addition to its parks, the city was home to well-curated museums, theaters, art galleries, a botanical garden, and more.

Arriving in June, we found that summer had settled in, with warm temperatures during the day that cooled down after sunset. The locals in Madrid were generally friendly and curious about Indians. Unlike some other Western European countries, they didn't exhibit an air of superiority. However, there was a language barrier as English was not widely understood or spoken, which sometimes posed communication challenges.

<u>Sagrada Familia</u>

We stayed at Plaza Luca de Tena, a central location in Madrid that made it convenient to travel anywhere in the city, including the museums, the bullet train station, and the stores. The Atocha Metro station, which was also the bullet train terminus, allowed us to easily explore other Spanish cities by train. Famous museums like the Reina Sofía and the Prado were only 15 minutes away from our accommodation. Gran Vía, the central street in Madrid, was a prime location where, especially on weekends, it seemed like the entire population of Madrid gathered. Street musicians would perform with full orchestras, creating an incredibly enjoyable atmosphere. During our visit to Gran Vía on a Saturday, I had an interesting experience when a Spanish girl with a loud makeup, dressed in a bikini, approached me for a selfie. I had to decline her offer due to my apprehensions as a foreigner. To reach Gran Vía, we only needed to take a 3-minute metro ride from our home station, Frontera.

Some of the must-see tourist destinations in Madrid include the Royal Palace, the Opera House, and more. The museum inside the Royal Palace is particularly noteworthy, showcasing excellent artifacts. Unfortunately, we missed out on witnessing the Flamenco dance, a popular Spanish cultural feature, as every venue we checked was fully sold.

One important thing I'd like to mention before I forget is that Eurail tickets can be booked in India itself if you plan your visits in advance. These trains are not only comfortable but also save you time, cruising at nearly 300 km per hour. Thanks to these high-speed trains, we were able to visit cities like Valencia, Barcelona, and Cordoba.

Our journey to outside towns from Madrid began with Toledo. We visited Toledo by an overland bus, which took about an hour and a half. The roads were incredibly smooth, nonbumpy, and flanked by farms.

Toledo is renowned for its synagogues, medieval cathedrals, and Alcazar (Military Museum). The city is situated on a hill, and in 2019, they installed an escalator in three stages to climb 1000 ft. From the hills, the view of Toledo on the ground was breathtaking. In the medieval period, Toledo served as the capital of Spain, and numerous structures stand as a testimony to this fact.

<u>Toledo, Spain</u>

Our next stop was Valencia. We traveled to this coastal city by bullet train from Atocha railhead, reaching there in two hours, although we missed our scheduled train by 15 minutes. At the seashore, many tourists and locals crowded for a swim on the weekend. My wife, Ajita, and our friend Krishna couldn't resist wetting their feet in the emerald blue waters of the Mediterranean.

<u>Royal Palace</u>

Our next destination was Cordoba, which we reached by bullet train, taking a little over two hours. We visited the famous Mezquita Church, which had served as a mosque during the medieval period before being captured by the Christians and converted into a church. The interior decoration and architectural features are so magnificent that they attract tourists from around the world. Cordoba was the city where street lights were first introduced. We tasted local Spanish cuisine, including a delicious vegetable stew, bread, and fish fry, which we thoroughly enjoyed. We also tried dishes like shangrilla, tapas, and pizza in Madrid.

Our final destination was Barcelona, the place associated with the legendary 2022 World Cup winner Messi. This city is known for its industrial prowess, and the wealthiest Spaniards are said to reside here, known as Catalonians. The world-famous Sagrada Familia Church has been under construction in this city for the last six centuries. Antoni Gaudí was the architect, and he happened to be a Catalonian. We visited the architect's house, designed and built by him, perched on a hill. Countless tourists gathered around this house to get a close look. Unfortunately, we couldn't get very close to Messi's house due to some ongoing demonstration. However, in front of the Barcelona Football Stadium, we saw a gigantic cutout of this world-famous football wizard.

With this, we concluded our journey in Spain and returned to India. The memories of this country will remain vivid forever.

AMAZING VISIT TO LIECHTENSTEIN AND SWITZERLAND

In 2005, during our European extravaganza trip with Thomas Cook, we had the opportunity to visit the wonderful and tiny country located between Austria and Switzerland, Liechtenstein. We reached there by an overland (Mercedes) bus from Swarovski in Austria. We explored both Vaduz, the capital, and the broader region of Liechtenstein. Unfortunately, it was a Sunday, so the vineyards in Vaduz were closed, and we missed the chance to visit a wine manufacturing factory.

Nevertheless, Liechtenstein more than made up for it with its stunning scenic beauty, offering breathtaking views of the Alpine range and a network of beautiful tree-lined streets. This tiny principality stretches for 25 km and is adorned with medieval castles. As of the 2021 census, it has a population of 39,039 people and covers an area of 160 sq. km. The official language spoken here is German.

During our visit to the city, we stopped by a retail store that primarily sold dress materials and souvenirs of the place. I remember buying a shirt, and the salesgirl led me to a deep basement fitting room, approximately 70 feet below ground level. When we entered the shop in a group of about 8 to 10 people, our loud chatter seemed to disturb the staff. They kindly reminded us, "Look, you guys are on vacation, but we are not," which naturally put an end to our chattering. We also enjoyed a tram tour of this picturesque city.

The locals, in general, appeared to be conservative, primarily due to the language barrier. It was fascinating to spend a couple of hours in a city so incredibly beautiful and with such a meagre population.

From Vaduz, we headed to Switzerland. As we approached the Swiss border, the Alpine mountain range, pine trees, and meadows opened up before us. We arrived at our hotel, Aupark, in Freiburg late in the evening. The following morning, after a hearty breakfast, we set off for Jungfrau, which stands at an altitude of 3,450 meters.

On our way, we passed through Interlaken and arrived in Lauterbrunnen by 9:30 am. From there, we took a cogwheeled train. This railway track up the hill was designed by Der Erbener, an engineer who unfortunately did not live to witness the inauguration of this challenging project that he successfully designed. In Jungfrau, we explored the Ice Palace, enduring freezing cold and snowfall on a September afternoon. Our lunch was delicious, featuring chicken and mashed potatoes accompanied by champagne. In the afternoon, we returned to Interlaken and refreshed ourselves with hot beverages and burgers at McDonald's.

The next morning, we embarked on a journey to Mount Titlis, which boasts of an altitude of 10,000 feet. We were fortunate to experience friendly, crisp weather with clear blue skies at the summit. We reached the top using a Roltair Pass, a revolving cable car, where our conductor happened to be an Indian girl. We had great fun on the mountain slopes, throwing snowballs and sliding down.

On our way back to the hotel, we visited the Trümmelbach Falls, the only glacial falls in Europe. In the evening, we explored Lucerne, cruising along the lake. Many of us indulged in souvenir shopping, including wristwatches and Swiss chocolates. Finally, as night fell, we returned to Zurich and checked into the Zurich Intercontinental Hotel, where we retired for the night.

Early the next morning, we explored Zurich city, cruised in the Rhine Falls, and visited the world-famous Lion sculpture carved out of stone. Thus, our visit to the wonderful country of Switzerland concluded in the Swiss capital.

Eighteen years have passed since we visited Liechtenstein, and the memories of this beautiful country still remain vivid in our minds.

SPARKLING SOUTH KOREA

In April 2015, I had the opportunity to visit the beautiful Asian country in the far east, and I am thankful to my wife and her two students from Mumbai's Amulakh School, Raj Mehta and Darsh Jain. These students had qualified in an online international gaming competition, earning them the chance to attend the Water Forum in South Korea. Under the guidance of their teacher, Ajita, they represented India in this competition when they were in the ninth grade.

The international Water Forum, held by K Water Academy in Tiajou, South Korea, was a significant event. It marked the first time an Indian school had participated in such a global gaming competition. Other participating countries included Singapore, Thailand, Taiwan, Hong Kong, Vietnam, China, Malaysia, and more. The Seventh World Water Forum which extended invitations to teachers and students from all of these countries and held it in Daegu, with 3,000 participants from around the world.

Our journey in South Korea began with an overland bus ride from Incheon Airport to K Water Academy in Daegu. The roads were smooth, and the surroundings were picturesque, making the two-hour journey quite pleasant. The accommodation provided by K Water Academy was excellent, comparable to

European standards. However, the food in South Korea was different from Indian cuisine, so we had to make some adjustments. The two students and Ajita managed with the food they brought from India.

One striking observation in South Korea was how meticulously they had built their infrastructure, despite gaining independence from Japan only in 1945, just two years before India. The parks, road layouts, hospitals, department stores, uniform building color schemes, and building heights were impressive. The infrastructure was designed with ample space, wide sidewalks that were not encroached upon, and dedicated green-marked cycle tracks on all roads. Visiting in the spring allowed us to enjoy the cherry blossoms and fully bloomed magnolias. The Koreans we encountered were not only friendly but also extremely disciplined.

We had the opportunity to travel on the Bullet Train KTX, which traveled at speed of up to 300 km per hour. This high-speed train took us from Don Daegu to Incheon in just one hour. An intriguing feature at train stations was the availability of toothpaste and toothbrushes for public use to maintain oral hygiene.

We also visited the Hyundai and Samsung factories, witnessing the gigantic scale of these famous car, truck, and electronic manufacturing biggies. Seoul, the capital of South Korea, left us enthralled with its meticulous preservation of historic monuments alongside modern urban infrastructure. One of the significant tourist attractions was Sunguyemun gate. Although our tour lasted just one week, the memories of historic locations in Seoul continue to be etched in our minds.

Before our return, we went back to Incheon and stayed in a hotel near the South China Sea. The entire hotel was practically empty, which created a somewhat eerie atmosphere. At night, aside from the sound of the sea waves, it was eerily quiet. The two students who accompanied Ajita were quite scared and not comfortable sleeping in their rooms alone. Let me describe the rooms that were booked for us. They had a ground floor with a sitting room featuring a wall-mounted TV, a narrow passage leading to the bathroom/toilet, and a kitchenette along the passage. There was a wooden ladder with rungs that led to a mezzanine floor where we slept at night. I had never stayed in such a hotel before, and I later learned that such types of hotels exist in Southeast Asia.

The next day, we reached Incheon International Airport in time to board our Korean Air flight to Bangkok. I must share my experience of flying with Korean Air. While in India, I met an elderly Parsi lady at the Korean Air office in Mumbai. When I inquired about this airline, she highly recommended it as she was a frequent flyer herself. I am thankful for her correct assessment because we have flown with many airlines, but the efficiency of the Korean Air crew on board was excellent. We had an overnight flight, and throughout the entire journey, the slim and agile flight attendants were prompt in attending to passengers' needs, which was something we had never seen before. I hope they are still maintaining their high standards.

Upon our return to Mumbai, we couldn't forget the Korean hospitality and the beauty of the country as a whole.

MEMORIES OF THE MIDDLE EAST

SEPTEMBER THE 11TH, 2001 - THE MIDDLE EAST PRE-9/11:

On September the 11th, 2001, the terrorist attack on the World Trade Centers in New York, along with other vital and prominent establishments in the United States, led to severe destabilization in the security landscape of the Middle East. The then-US president declared war against the Middle East, primarily targeting Iraq, as they believed the country was harboring Weapons of Mass Destruction (WMD). This resulted in extensive bombing campaigns across Iraq. Later, it was realized that these claims were not accurate. However, the destruction continued, devastating the Middle Eastern region, with countries like Syria and Lebanon also affected.

Witnessing such atrocities that destroyed the lives of innocent people is truly distressing. The initial retaliation by US authorities seemed never-ending, creating the seeds of enmity and leading to an increase in terrorist attacks in European countries. Restoring peace became an increasingly challenging task.

I would rather cherish the memories of the Middle East that I had experienced prior to 9/11 during my time in Iraq and Iran.

MEMORIES OF IRAQ:

In 1979-80, I was assigned to an electricity infrastructure project in Baghdad, Iraq, in a joint venture between Tata and Mitsubishi from India and Japan. During this period, I had the opportunity to interact with locals, including Kurds, Armenians, and Jews. While the Jews were somewhat reserved due to strained political relations, interactions with others were enriching. In my free time, I explored various places in the country, including Babylon (home to the Hanging Gardens, a UNESCO World Heritage Site), Mosul, Kut, and Samarra.

Baghdad, an exotic city, situated on the banks of the Tigris River, that meets the Euphrates River in the south. It featured famous 5-star hotels in upscale districts like Sadoon Street, while Rashid Street had eateries and nightclubs like Moulin Rouge and Lido. Only foreigners with passports were allowed entry to these nightclubs, and I had the chance to visit Moulin Rouge, where I witnessed an Egyptian belly dancer named Nadia Omer, known for her performances in Paris and Baghdad. Iraqi kebabs were delectable, and during that time, Iraq was the world's third-largest date producer, offering juicy dates at very affordable prices. The exchange rate was such that one Iraqi Dinar was equal to INR 32.

Lamb's meat was readily available and delicious. Saddam Hussein was the controversial Iraqi President at the time, with mixed opinions about his leadership.

The climate in Iraq is tropical, with pleasant weather between November and March, while the summer months in July and August saw temperatures soar to 50°C, sometimes accompanied by sandstorms.

I recall the friendly nature of the local communities in Iraq, which had historical ties as Indian soldiers fought for Iraq during World War II. One of our senior colleagues had also fought in Iraq during that time.

My prayers go out for the return of normalcy to Iraq, allowing its people to live in peace without fear.

MEMORIES OF IRAN: (1985- '87)

As mentioned earlier, we were in Iran during the war, which brought us face to face with danger on numerous occasions. I will share some of these unforgettable experiences.

Tehran

Once, near the Indian school where my wife, Ajita, and our children were studying, extensive Iraqi bombing took place. This attack aimed to target the nearby US Embassy but had the potential to harm our family. Thankfully, they all remained unharmed.

On another occasion, while we were hosting a dinner party at our apartment, about 500 meters away from our home in Tehran's Swed Khandan locality, Iraqi forces bombed the area. The explosion was so powerful that our entire apartment shook as if there was a massive earthquake. In the kitchen, a pressure cooker bounced off the floor, and my son was so frightened that he bit his tongue until it bled. We had Iranian women, my wife's colleagues and schoolteachers, as our guests that evening. After the party, they bade us goodbye and drove back to their homes. Iranian women were known for being skilled drivers. We kept our radios/transistors on to listen for the siren warnings transmitted during attacks.

<u>Tehran Home</u>

During one attack, I was at the Medune Vanak office in Tehran when Iraqi warplanes invaded. We would rush to the basement for safety during these incidents. Over the course of this decade-long war, nearly 10 million lives were lost.

We also went to visit the Caspian Sea, the world's largest lake, covering one-third of the Earth's surface water. We stayed in a seaside hotel in Rasht city near the Caspian Sea during the winter season, and it was bitterly cold. Unfortunately, the room heater didn't work, adding to our discomfort. We tasted delicious local produce like boiled beetroot, and we savored the mouthwatering "Chelo Kebab" during dinner.

In 2013, while in transit from Rome to Mumbai via Istanbul, we met an Iranian family. The head of the family was traveling from Toronto to Tehran and shared that Iran had made significant progress, improving infrastructure with projects like the Metro, roads, and railways to enhance mobility for Iranians. He even extended an invitation for us to visit Tehran.

I must recount a unique experience. We were invited to the Indian Ambassador's residence, hosted by Ambassador R. M. Gokhale, along with Tata engineers and their families in Tehran's diplomatic enclave of Farmanieh. During this event, we had the opportunity to mingle with Iranians in their colorful normal attire, without the traditional "Manto" (overcoat) that covers a woman's body. They looked beautiful and vividly colorful. The function proceeded smoothly, but towards the end, Iranian Revolutionary

Guards (Pazdars) forcibly attempted to enter the premises to arrest Iranian women who had disregarded the approved dress code. The Indian Ambassador intervened, warning the guards that their intrusion was unauthorized, and they subsequently withdrew.

Later, an Iranian family from Tehran visited Mumbai and met us. Memories of the Iranian people, Tehran, delicious Iranian cuisine, and the beauty of the country remain vivid in our minds. Tehran is situated at the foothills of the Elburz Mountains, offering breathtaking scenery, and the people were incredibly friendly. My wife and children made many friends and even learned the Persian language.

It saddens us to read about the challenges faced by women in Iran today, contrasting with the friendly and colorful memories we hold from our time there.

ENCHANTING SLOVENIA CROATIA AND BOSNIA

TRIP PLANNING

The proposal for this short yet intense trip to the countries located on the eastern side of the Adriatic Sea came from one of our European friends, the proprietor of an aircraft parts manufacturing firm in Dresden, East Germany. He explicitly informed us that these countries are stunningly beautiful, offering a diverse range of natural features.

Dubrovnik

In the past, Yugoslavia disintegrated into several countries, namely Slovenia, Croatia, and Bosnia-Herzegovina. So, we began the process of obtaining visas, starting with Slovenia. However, we initially encountered a setback when we were asked to visit the Consulate of Slovenia in New Delhi. We objected to this and, as a result, a Vice Consul based in Mumbai, our home city, suggested that we should contact the Consul General in New Delhi. Our travel history in Europe was digitally shared with the Consul General via VFS in Mumbai. After reviewing our extensive European travels, the Consul General readily agreed to issue the visas. With this green signal, we set off for Slovenia.

SLOVENIA

In 2017, on June the 7th, we flew off on a Swiss Air flight to Zurich en route to Ljubljana, the Slovenian capital. Upon our arrival at the small airport in Jože Pučnik, Ljubljana, we were greeted by our Tour Director, Suleiman Oki, who would guide us for the next 7 days as part of the Cosmos Travels group. The airport was situated in a valley surrounded by hills, offering a refreshing and soothing environment that relieved our travel fatigue. Our entire tour group, consisting of Americans, Australians, Europeans, South Americans, and the two of us from India, was waiting on the Cosmos bus.

Our hotel in the city, the M Hotel, was 24 km from the airport. Along the way, we were treated to picturesque green surroundings with meadows. At that time, Ljubljana had a population of 300,000. The city's air was crisp and completely unpolluted, with greenery all around. There were several historic monuments for tourists to visit, including the triple bridges and a Roman Catholic Church, which were must-see attractions. The church's Alpine architecture was particularly appealing. We observed that the locals were very friendly, and English was easily understood and spoken by them, making communication a breeze.

<u>Postojna Caves</u>

One of Slovenia's must-visit tourist spots was the Postojna Caves. The cave system stretched for 20 km, and for the first 6 km, visitors could enjoy a meter gauge open-car train ride, which was a delightful experience. As we ventured deeper into the cool caves, we marveled at the stalactites, the stalagmites, and various shapes formed by the frozen elements. Our female guide shared an intriguing historical tidbit with us – during World War II, Adolf Hitler, the formidable German Chancellor, stored fuel in this cave for military use. However, it was later destroyed by Austro-Hungarian forces, thwarting Hitler's war plans.

CROATIA

To the south of Slovenia lies Croatia, a stunningly beautiful country situated along the coast of the Adriatic Sea. Previously, when we visited Venice in Italy, we were captivated by its coastal charm on the western side of the Adriatic Sea. However, upon reaching Croatia, particularly in Split and Dubrovnik, we were completely enamored. As we ventured to the coast, the clean emerald-green waters of the Adriatic Sea greeted us. These places were in no way inferior to Venice or other Italian coastal towns. Along the Zadar coast, we found that concrete aprons were built in such a way, with embedded pipes, that these pipes acted like musical instruments, producing soothing music as sea waves entered and exited. It was a unique natural musical experience, and any world-class musician would appreciate this place. The entire coastline of

Dubrovnik was surrounded by hills made of limestone deposits, milky white and shimmering in the sunlight.

In Dubrovnik, due to its intrinsic natural beauty, numerous famous Hollywood films were shot on location. In January 2017, the year of our visit, Leonardo DiCaprio starred in "Robin Hood," which was filmed here. Our guide informed us that DiCaprio fell in love with this place so much that he stayed for a fortnight after filming. He immersed himself in the beauty of the location and the friendly people.

<u>Split</u>

Dubrovnik boasts of the Franciscan Monastery, Rector's Palace, and other Roman-built historic monuments that endured the ravages of war. We took a cable car ride, converting our Euros into the local Croatian currency, which provided us with a breathtaking view of the entire coast, city, and the Adriatic Sea. From the Cable Car station at the top, there was a restaurant for refreshments. From our Tirena Hotel, we could access Copacabana Beach, where sun loungers were available for tourists to relax. We took a powered boat ride, during which we observed locals sunbathing on the undulating coast, some of them unclothed. Ajita pointed this out, and our tour mates rushed to our side with their telephoto lenses, nearly upsetting the balance of the boat. While boating, we saw the city of Dubrovnik, which had grown on terraces due to the hilly terrain. The beach had a pebbly surface, which meant fewer beachgoers.

SPLIT

Split is another popular tourist destination in Croatia. Here, a Roman play was staged by local actors every afternoon, a tradition we didn't want to miss. However, our tour guide cautioned us about the Romanians in the crowd, who were known pickpockets. The girls would come very close, scantily dressed, to divert attention and then rob unsuspecting tourists. As you approach the shore, a very high stone wall, the boundary wall of the Roman Palace, comes into view. In prehistoric times, guards used to watch for enemy movements from this vantage point. We enjoyed some Gelato (ice cream), which reminded us of our visits to Rome, Florence, Venice, Pisa, and other Italian cities. I recall an incident where an absent-minded Australian tourist in our group lost his passport here and couldn't accompany us for the rest of the tour.

Croatia's national treasure, Plitvice Park, was another place we visited. We explored it via a special train and then trekked through the park. It featured many waterfalls of different heights. The excellent maintenance of the entire park impressed us, and we trekked for almost five hours in the crisp and unpolluted surroundings with minimal fatigue.

BOSNIA AND HERZEGOVINA

Tiny, beautiful Mostar, an old medieval town, is set in the rugged and extraordinarily beautiful Neretva river valley. During the medieval period, this country was mainly ruled by the Turkish. A few years ago, the beautiful single-arch stone bridge that connects both shores on opposite sides of the river was rebuilt, standing as a symbol of unity. During the 1990s, signs of war damage on buildings and historic monuments testified to the intensity of the war. The architecture and designs of the buildings in this region bear the marks of Turkish rule, resembling traditional Turkish styles in design and architectural patterns. It reminded us of our trip to Istanbul, where we saw similar architectural patterns in buildings, mosques, and edifices. The lacework and women's clothing, such as blouses and gowns, followed Muslim styles. Many intricate women's accessories were on display, particularly attracting female tourists. We purchased tablecloths with lace and children's toys made from used bullets.

<u>Dubrovnik</u>

Before visiting Mostar, we stopped in Sarajevo, the capital of Bosnia, where we spent a night at the Bosnia Hotel. This city has hosted the Winter Olympics. During our walk along the streets, we saw several cathedrals, churches, and mosques. We witnessed a historically significant street junction, where our guide pointed out that this was where the then-Yugoslavian President Ferdinand Archibald was assassinated. He had come to this city with his pregnant wife, and both were killed by assassins. This incident triggered the First World War, and the street junction became an important historic site for all tourists to visit.

From here, we began our journey back to Slovenia and reached Zagreb. This city resembles Prague, with its red-tiled, sloping-roofed houses. We explored the streets of Zagreb and came across a unique museum where lovers who had failed to click romantically would donate their used belongings and articles for display. The fruit market in Zagreb was excellent. We also saw a church with architectural designs reminiscent of the Hungarian style, featuring beautiful mosaic tiles throughout.

Finally, we set off for Ljubljana. Along the way, as we crossed territorial boundaries, we noticed that the border checkpoints were under strict scrutiny. They checked everyone's passports and travel documents thoroughly. It seemed that territorial sovereignty was well-guarded at that time. Thus, our week-long tour of Slavic countries came to an end, leaving us with vivid memories.

ISTANBUL

As avid travelers, we had long wished to visit the exotic and historic city of Istanbul. The day our wish came true, and we obtained our online visa (thanks to having a valid US visa) to travel to this city, our joy knew no bounds. Back in 2014, this city, with a population of 17 million, attracted global travelers due to its unique geographical location. The Bosphorus Strait divides the city into two halves: the Asian continent on one side and Europe on the other. Consequently, the city's culture is a unique blend of these two continents.

Blue Mosque

On May 1st, we arrived via Turkish Airlines at Kemal Ataturk Airport. In 2014, upon our arrival, we discovered that there was a public demonstration going on in Taksim Square, near our intended residence. Due to this, airport officials suggested that we find a hotel close to the airport for that day. In the process, we had to search for a hotel in various parts of Istanbul, and we finally secured temporary accommodation in an area that we later realized was in a red-light district. So, we returned to the airport region and ultimately booked a stay at the Holiday Inn hotel for three days.

Hagia Sophia

Later, we reached our scheduled Entis apartment in the upscale Beyoglu district, close to Taksim Square and just one street away from Istiklal Caddesi street. Istiklal Caddesi was possibly one of the world's most pedestrianized streets, bustling with tourists from around the world and alive until 2 am in the morning. It was lined with famous retail outlets, eateries like McDonald's, KFC, French perfume shops, renowned clothing shops, watch shops, and street singers. Watching the ice cream shop owners' playful pranks with customers was a fun sight. Restaurants were full, and a red tramcar ferried tourists. We enjoyed a meal at a restaurant hosted by our friends, Senguptas, where the fish fry and curry were excellent and simply mouthwatering. Turkish kebabs (locally called Kebap) were a delight, and continental food was delicious too. Eateries welcomed guests from different parts of the world. Foodies savored baked chestnuts and Bivalve with lemon juice. Baklava and Gauze were excellent sweets that anyone would relish. The red tram, as mentioned earlier, was an attractive mode of transportation, taking tourists deep into the city's alleys. Istanbul had numerous outlets for converting other currencies into Turkish Lira. We carried Euros, the exchange rate was 1 Euro=30 TL .

<u>Grand Bazar</u>

Modern developments in the city attracted tourists. We traveled by a funicular from Taksim to Kavatas in just 15 seconds. Alongside these modern aspects, the city scrupulously maintained its medieval monuments. A cruise along the Bosphorus was a must, offering breathtaking coastal views of Asia to the north and Europe to the south. Night cruises featured belly dancing and Turkish cultural programs.

<u>Bosphorus Strait</u>

Other must-visit tourist spots included the Yerebatan Cistern, Grand Bazaar, Topkapi Palace, Zero Point, and the Blue Mosque. Istanbul's famous Turkish culture and mouthwatering culinary delights left an unforgettable impression, making it one of the world's top tourist destinations.

Our visits in this unique city began with the Grand Bazaar, built in 1461 but still impeccably maintained. The market comprised 1,000 shops offering various items, including glassware, carpets, clothing, electronic gadgets, Turkish delights, sweets, kebabs, and more. We marveled at the Izmic Tile work, with its visually delightful blue design. Zafran was renowned but prohibitively expensive. Many Hollywood films, including James Bond, were shot on location in this remarkable city.

A few interesting facts about the Grand Bazaar: It's impossible to cover the entire market in one day due to its vastness. Shop owners warmly welcome visitors, treating them as if they've known each other for ages and often gladly posing for pictures with tourists.

Some other notable tourist spots in Istanbul are the Blue Mosque, Hagia Sophia (pronounced as Aya Sofia), and the Yerebatan Cistern. Aya Sofia, originally built in 300 AD under the rule of Constantinople, underwent significant improvements in 500 AD during the time of Theodesius. It was initially a mosque but later converted into a church by Christians. The interiors of Aya Sofia are beautifully decorated. One of its main attractions is a massive marble vessel dating from 4 BC to 3 BC, during the Hellenistic period. This historic site also houses the well preserved Kabba Stone, a sacred artifact that we were fortunate enough to touch.

The Yerebatan Cistern is an underground water storage tank with a treatment facility that serves as the water source for Istanbul. Water is collected through conduits running from the Belgrade Forest to the city, a system established by the Roman Emperor Justinian between 527 AD and 565 AD.

Sultanahmet

Topkapi Palace, also known as the Cannon Gate, holds significant historical and religious importance in Turkey. Zero Point is another location believed to be the center point of the planet, established by the Romans before the birth of Christ. We also visited Miniaturk, a park showcasing miniature models of historic places in Istanbul, located in an hour's drive from the city center. This park is a favorite spot among children and offers various games. The entry fee was TL 10 per person.

One morning, our Turkish host invited us for breakfast in the upscale Istanbul beachfront suburb of Bebek, which was a visual delight. The houses in this area were built on terraced lands on hilly terrain, and it's reported to be one of the costliest neighborhoods in Europe. We visited a beautiful park adjacent to the restaurant, Laleh, known for its red tulip flowers. We also witnessed a cable-stayed single-span bridge built by the Japanese engineers across the Bosphorus Strait, connecting both shores—a true engineering marvel indeed.

We frequently used the funicular to travel to Sultanahmet, where most historic monuments are located. Unlike some Middle Eastern countries like Iran or Iraq, Turkish women do not completely cover themselves from head to foot. Instead, they dress more similarly to European women. While communicating with locals, one could manage conversations in broken English. We also picked up some Turkish words from our hotel concierge staff, such as "Be" for men and "Beyan" for women. Some words in Turkish resembled those in Bengali. In Turkish language, "Gunaidiyan" means "Good Morning." We had the opportunity to witness Sufi dancing in a restaurant in Sultanahmet, which is a form of religious dancing. The musical instruments used during Sufi dancing are known as "Kanu" and "Def." Officially, Turkey is now called "Turkiyeh." We even spotted the shooting location of a popular Bengali film in front of the Blue Mosque.

Before our trip to Istanbul, many of our friends thought that a period of 11 days was too long to spend there. However, my wife and I soon realized that this exotic city had so much to offer that the duration as envisaged fell too short. We had to skip visiting many tourist spots due to time constraints. During this tour, our daughter, her family, and our friends Krishna and Syamal Sengupta added more joy to our travel experiences.

A VISIT TO NIAGARA FALLS

Our friends and family members repeatedly reminded us not to leave the United States without visiting Niagara Falls. Niagara Falls is surrounded by the meadows of Buffalo State Forest region to the north, in upstate New York. We started from Somerset, New Jersey, at 7:30 pm on the way to Rochester to my nephew's home, driven by our son. The nighttime drive through the Pocono Mountain region in dense fog was indeed quite challenging as the fog lamps could not serve their intended purpose. Our seven-and-a-half-hour drive that night was far from pleasant. Being completely fatigued, we rested that night at my nephew's house in Rochester. It was decided that the next afternoon, we would set off for Niagara. On a Friday at 4:30 pm, we started by road, covering 50 miles until we finally reached Niagara Park. Upon reaching the park, we were amazed by the lush green meadows all around, soothing our eyes. On the way, as we approached the Buffalo airport region, the meadows greeted us.

The double-decked Niagara Boat is named the "Maid of the Mist." This boat took us to the bottom of the gigantic falls. We were very lucky that day as the park attendant indicated that the last trip was on, so we needed to hurry up not to miss it. They provided us with blue disposable overall aprons to save our dresses from getting completely drenched, as the wind was quite strong. Indeed, with the water vapor, the water drops from the falls created a dense, foggy environment, which was a once-in-a-lifetime experience. One more thing I wish to share is that the elevator we took to reach the bottom moved with breakneck speed, a bit scary, but it was safely operated at a speed of 500 feet per minute. Water splashed from an altitude of 200 feet with a gushing speed, creating lots of froth at the bottom and water droplets all around. Niagara is a Red Indian name, and many establishments, states, and significantly important places are named after Red Indians. Many years ago, the first hydel power station was founded here. 2009 population in this region was 53,000, quite meager compared to the sprawling area. As we reached the crest of Niagara, we could clearly see Ontario, the border town located in Canada. We could see the houses, the roads, and the cars moving about. We even spotted a bridge connecting the US with Canada, guarded by the security personnel on either end. The enchanting memories of Niagara are still vivid in our minds.

BRANDENBERG ROYALS-THE CRYPT

During our second trip to Berlin, we received an intriguing offer from our German host, Thomas Warnatsch. He informed us that he could arrange a visit to the crypt under the famous Berlin Cathedral, located on the banks of the Spree River. Without hesitation, we accepted this opportunity, and it turned out to be one of the most thrilling experiences of our week-long tour in the German Democratic Republic (GDR) capital.

This royal burial site was situated next to Lustgarten Cathedral, where the Hohenzollern cemetery was also located. To reach the royal burial chambers, we descended 100 meters (327 feet) below ground level. Upon arrival, we were greeted by an eerie atmosphere — very dimly lit, extremely cool, and profoundly silent. The realization that these royals had rested here for centuries sent shivers down our spines. The crypt housed the remains of 94 royals, born between the 16th and 20th centuries. During this period, the Brandenburg Royals gained fame for their Prussian historical and cultural contributions.

In 2011, during our stay in Dresden, we embarked on a journey to Berlin in a BMW car driven by our German host, Thomas', who owned an aircraft parts manufacturing unit in Hidanu Sud, just a 10-minute surface rail ride from Hopt Ban Hoff, Dresden. Our son-in-law worked as an engineer in his firm. This tour included Ajita, my wife, our daughter Arpita, and our grandson Arnab. Thomas' drove us to Berlin using a shorter route, and we reached speeds of up to 200 km/hr. Thanks to Thomas' for special permit, we were granted permission to visit this crypt, which is typically not accessible to regular tourists. Thomas' long-standing acquaintance with the Cathedral Cardinal facilitated our unique visit to this royal burial site.

The Berlin Cathedral (Dom Kirsche, as known locally) was our first stop before entering the crypt. The burial site contains the remains of 94 different German royals who lived between the 16th and 20th centuries, including members of various royal clans. The wooden coffins were meticulously engraved with the names of the royals and were flawlessly maintained. The quality of the wood was exceptional, without any blemishes, showcasing the professionalism of the maintenance team. The coffins featured immaculate velvet and brocade work. We were overwhelmed, standing among the remains of German royals who had ruled this advanced European nation for five centuries. Among the notable burials were those of Hohenzollern, Frederick the Second, and Johan Cicero, who played significant roles in introducing Prussian culture.

The coffins followed the Gothic style of fabrication, and being in their presence made us feel as though we were amid these royals of the past. This unique experience left a lasting impression on us, and the memories are vivid even today.

During World War II, the burial place of the Hohenzollerns suffered damage due to the collapse of the cathedral's main dome. It took considerable time to restore the site. Finally, on November 20, 1999, this royal crypt was ceremoniously reopened.

The maintenance of the royal crypt has been entrusted to a professionally managed organization, ensuring that it is preserved traditionally, following the methods used for centuries. The meticulous maintenance and preservation of this historic site are a testament to the dedication and care given to this important part of Germany's cultural heritage.

Our visit to the royal crypt lasted an hour, but the memories are as fresh as ever.

BEGUILING VOLLENDAM & AMSTERDAM

In 2005, we embarked on an extensive overland journey through Western Europe, starting from the south in Italy and then moving through Austria, Germany, Belgium, Switzerland, the Netherlands, France, and concluding our adventure in the UK, in London.

During our travels, we reached Amsterdam, and from there, we made our way to Vollendam, a unique fishing harbor that shares a geographic connection with Coventry. To provide context for Vollendam, it's important to mention a bit about Amsterdam. This city lies below sea level for approximately two-thirds of its area, but ingenious engineering has ensured that it remains afloat, defying the surrounding sea.

While in Amsterdam, we had the opportunity to witness Schiphol Airport from a unique perspective. As we approached the airport, we were surprised to see an aircraft seemingly taking off from a motorable road in the distance. However, as we got closer, we realized that a section of the runway built high over the road.

Our Amsterdam visit included stops at a Cheese factory and a wooden shoe shop. My wife, Ajita, even engaged with a Dutch shoemaker to craft a personalized shoe, which she cherished. We also had the chance to visit the world-famous Nestle factory. The city itself boasts numerous canals, and we noticed that tourists often explored the city by glass-topped boats, admiring buildings with chain pulleys on their upper beams, designed to lift loads to upper floors externally. We also visited the Anne Frank House, where Anne Frank, a Jewish girl, initially escaped Hitler's persecution but tragically could not evade his later attacks. Her diary remains a universally acclaimed literary work. A canal cruise is a must when visiting a city known for its intricate network of canals. As we ventured into rural areas, we noticed that farmers here owned cars and tractors, and we encountered numerous huge cows, as this region is renowned for its dairy products. We also marveled at the iconic windmills and the vibrant blooming tulip fields.

Our journey led us to Madurodam, a unique attraction showcasing miniature models of landmarks, including cathedrals, football pitches, railway stations, windmills, and more, all meticulously crafted to scale.

Subsequently, we made our way to Vollendam, a historic fishing harbor within the municipality of Edam-Vollendam. Here, we had the opportunity to taste freshly smoked raw trout fish. Vollendam's existence as a harbor dates back to 1357. During our September visit, we experienced the chilly weather typical of the North Sea region. We also encountered unique seabirds, and the current population of this charming place is reported to be 22,715. Memories of Vollendam continue to linger in our hearts and minds.

OUR LONDON VISIT

In September 2005, on the 19th, we arrived at Gare Du Nord station in Paris at 8:30 am to board the London-bound Eurostar train, embarking on our first journey through the Channel Tunnel. At 10:15 am, the train began its journey, and a group of us Indians, traveling with Thomas Cook, an international tour operator, couldn't contain our excitement. The train's destination was Waterloo Station, a two-hour journey covering a distance of 400 km.

As scheduled, we reached Waterloo and were greeted by an overland bus that transported us to the Novotel Hotel in New Hampshire, where we had reservations for our stay in London.

This vibrant city, founded by the Romans 2000 years ago, is often considered one of the most exciting on the planet. We were fortunate to have relatives living in Old Windsor who kindly invited us to stay with them, in proximity to the world-famous Royal Windsor Castle. We took the tube to Hounslow, where our relative had his Lexus parked, ready to drive us to their home. After a quick refreshment, we set off to visit Windsor Castle, a place where, as per my nephew, Her Majesty the Queen would drive herself to spend her weekends.

During our London city tour, we explored various attractions including Kensington Palace, where Princess Diana resided. We also visited the residence of Indian steel magnate Mittal, and our tour guide even pointed out Sir Elton John's mansion. In London, places such as Albert Memorial Hall, the London Natural History Museum, London Science Museum, Victoria Museum, Hyde Park, Madam Tussaud Wax Museum, Big Ben, the UK Parliament, Buckingham Palace (the royal residence), Piccadilly Circus, and more are well worth a visit.

Our visit to the wax museum was especially memorable. The lifelike statues of celebrities, members of the Royal family, sports stars, and world-famous politicians like Martin Luther King and J.F. Kennedy left us feeling as if they were genuinely present. The statue of Marilyn Monroe was particularly astonishing, and visitors could be seen taking photos alongside these remarkable figures. We also visited the Chamber of Horrors, providing a spine-chilling experience by illustrating the darkest stories of London's history.

A spectacular ride on the London Eye offered breathtaking views of the city. Oxford Street, another must-visit location, is one of the world's most elegant shopping districts where we enjoyed some shopping, albeit briefly, due to time constraints.

We took a surface train to visit our niece's house in Croydon, Surrey, a suburb of London.

In summary, London is a city that encompasses all the elements of an elite metropolis. One of the highlights of our London experience was the ease of communication.

Our visit to London concluded in just three days, and we flew back to Mumbai via Milan on an Italian airline, Alitalia. To this day, the memories of our 2005 visit to London remain vivid.

OUR US SOJOURN IN 2009

Our son, Arjun, was posted in the United States at that time. He had been scheduled for this posting, and once he got settled there, he invited us to visit the US and stay with them. Thanks to his letter of invitation and being an employee of a renowned US-based IT company, we obtained multiple-entry and exit visas that were valid for ten years. The US Consulate staff in Mumbai found it surprising that we had visited so many European countries but hadn't yet been to the US.

<u>USA philadelphia</u>

At the end of May, we boarded a wide-bodied Air India aircraft in Mumbai, which was already packed as this flight originated from Ahmedabad. Finally, we arrived at Newark Airport in New Jersey, where our son and daughter-in-law, Shriya, came to receive us. They were living in Somerset, NJ, at that time. Somerset was a very quiet and peaceful neighborhood predominantly occupied by white Americans. On the day we arrived, Arjun took us to Atlantic City, famous for its casinos crowded with gamblers.

New York

After that, we visited Jersey City, where we took a cruise along the Hudson River. The New York City skyline was a visual delight, and we got very close to the Statue of Liberty, which had been damaged during the 9/11 terrorist attack.

Later, on a weekend, we traveled from the Path station to New York City. Our friends, Syamal and Krishna Sengupta, who were living there, took us to the world-famous Metropolitan Museum, Liberty

Natural Museum, and St. Paul's Cathedral. This church, although close to the World Trade Center, remained intact during the devastating attack.

Subsequently, Krishna drove us in her Lexus car to Washington, where Krishna and Syamal had booked us to stay at Dulles, in the Hyatt Hotel. From our room, the runway was clearly visible, allowing us to watch endless landings and departures of aircraft. We visited Washington's landmarks, such as the Potomac River and the famous Smithsonian Museum, wherein the first aircraft designed by the Wright Brothers was displayed. Speaking of the Wright Brothers, I'd like to share their intriguing comments about why no one could invent an aircraft before them. We also witnessed American Independence Day celebrations, where ex-US Army Marines were seen riding huge Harley Davidson bikes on the highways, making it an unforgettable sight.

For anyone visiting New York, not coming to Times Square would make their visit to the US incomplete. Times Square is such a vibrant city center that might not be found anywhere else on this planet. It could be the most pedestrianized location in the world, where people from a variety of cultures, appearances, religions, attire, languages, and more can be witnessed. In one of the streets closed to traffic, chairs are set up so that people visiting this place can take a break and immerse themselves in the unique city ambience.

My wife, Ajita, went with my cousin sister, Ratna Sharma, to visit some schools in New York City. They are childhood friends and studied in the same school, and they are not only relatives but also very good friends. In the science sections of New York schools, Ajita gained valuable experience by observing their teaching methods.

Atlantic Coast

On the way to visiting the Niagara Falls, we stayed overnight at our nephew Indrajit's home located in Rochester, upstate New York. We thoroughly enjoyed our stay there.

Afterward, we went to Wayne, where our other nephew, Ashish, and his wife Ruby were living with their family. We stayed with them for two days, and during our visit, we went to the Atlantic seacoast for a picnic. Ashish also hosted a grand lunch party for us.

During our stay in Wayne, we visited Shepherd Lake, wherein the natural beauty of this place left us spellbound. Later, we visited Philadelphia, where one of Ajita's school students was settled. We stayed with them for a night, and the next day, along with Ajita's other school friends who had gathered there, we went on a Duck Bus ride on the Delaware River.

Thus, our six-week-long trip to the US came to an end. The memories of our tour are still vivid, and we often mentally revisit those moments.

A DAY IN BRUSSELS

In 2005, in mid-September, we traveled to Brussels, the capital city of Belgium. We left Cologne in the morning and reached the city by an overland bus, covering a distance of 500 km. We were excited about visiting the city that is famous for being associated with Tintin. Hergé, the creator of Tintin, was from Belgium.

During the 12th, 13th, and 14th centuries, Brussels grew to become one of the major towns in the Duchy of Brabant. Its economic mainstay was the manufacturing of luxury fabrics, which were exported to Paris, Venice, and the Champagne region of France. Later, Brussels became one of the richest cities in Europe. The NATO headquarters and the EU Commission are located here. The locals predominantly speak Flemish, which is equivalent to Dutch.

In Brussels, tourists from all over the world visit the GRAND PLACE, where flower shows are held, and twice a year, flower carpets are prepared and displayed.

The Manneken-Pis fountain (1619), an all-bronze statue of a boy urinating openly and endlessly, is another famous attraction. It's located in an alley, and this boy is often referred to as the oldest citizen of the city. Brussels is also famous as the headquarters of the European Commission, making it a true global city. As the seat of the "EU," it's known as the capital of Europe. The city covers a geographical area of 62 sq. miles (161 sq. km) with a population estimated at 1.2 million in 2022. The city experiences seasonal rainfall of 810 mm, with snowfall occurring only two or three times a year, and average temperatures ranging between 20 to 25 degrees Celsius.

The city welcomes visitors with landmarks like the Grand Place, Central Market, and Town Hall. We took some photos in the Grand Place and also did some shopping in the nearby market where Moroccans and Tunisians were selling garments. We also tasted the famous Brussels waffles and purchased a lot of dark Belgian chocolates.

The Atomium is another intriguing tourist spot where one can observe an atom enlarged by 1.65 lakh times. Many World Trade Fairs in Europe are held here.

Our guide at the time informed us that many Indian diamond merchants conduct their diamond business in Brussels. A particular Indian community was known for their involvement in this business.

We should also mention Adolphe Sax, who created the musical wind instrument, the Saxophone. The town where Adolphe was born is adorned with sculptures of Saxophones. The Saxophone plays a vital role in many musical concerts.

Our visit to Brussels concluded, but the memories continue to occupy our minds to this day.

ENCHANTING PORTUGAL SOJOURN

At last, on June 13th, 2023, in the afternoon, we landed at Aeroporto Portela, the one and only airport in Lisbon (Lisboa). We realized that we had reached the country we had planned to visit when our friends Krishna and Syamal Sengupta invited us to stay with them in the Portuguese capital. We took a cab and reached the apartment they had booked for us at Rua Mirante 31 in half an hour. This apartment was conveniently located close to Santa Apolonia rail/metro station and in the proximity of San Vicen Church.

In the afternoon, we went to Graca, where we encountered a mixed crowd of tourists and locals enjoying a music festival in a street square. We had Shangrila, a cocktail made with red wine, crushed strawberries, and other ingredients—a very soothing and tasty drink. We also enjoyed "Chamoches" (samosas), which were deliciously stuffed with boiled chicken.

OCEANARIUM

We visited the Oceanarium, a sprawling aquarium displaying a variety of ocean flora and fauna. We were completely spellbound by the numerous rare sea species, including sharks, seahorses, penguins, arctic puffins, amphibians, corals, jellyfish, and a replica of the Amazon rainforest. They even showed us in an audiovisual auditorium how different foods were meticulously prepared and fed to various creatures during scheduled feeding times. Everywhere we looked, the aquarium was excellently maintained, and Portugal can boast of having one of the finest facilities among European countries.

ALFAMA

Alfama was very close to our place, and we could explore its undulating topography on foot. It is an elevated area that offers a breathtaking bird's eye view from the viewing gallery. The sloping red-roofed houses with the backdrop of the Tagus River and the Atlantic Ocean in the distance were simply awe-inspiring. Even a photograph of this place would testify to its beauty.

RESTORADOUR (RESTORER)

We visited this place by taking an underground metro from Santa Apolonia. It was a large square surrounded by open-air restaurants, boutiques, souvenir shops, and more. The square was bustling with tourists, locals, and passersby. We savored Nata (egg tarts), codfish fry, burgers, and delicious Portuguese cuisine. The Bangladeshi-owned souvenir shops did brisk business as their prices were reasonable, and buyers could haggle for further discounts. For those with a sweet tooth, reasonably priced chocolate pastries from the Pastelerias were a delight.

PALACE

The Lisbon Palace was built in the 19th century and is a neoclassical monument in the civil parish of Ajuda in central Portugal. I want to share an incident that occurred while we were taking a break in a restaurant near the Palace. As I tried to place an empty bottle (UKAL) on the table, it slipped and fell to the floor. To our surprise, the entire restaurant crowd started clapping, as if Ronaldo had scored a goal. However, the owner of the restaurant explained that it was a sign of good luck, which is why I received such applause. My trip to Portugal continued to go very well. Another intriguing piece of information I must share is that while trekking down the Pombal region, an upscale district of Lisbon, a local pointed out an apartment in a building owned by Ronaldo, which he had purchased for 7 million Euros.

MIRADOURO SANTA LUZIA

We visited the castle (Castelo) past the sparse ruins of the Roman Theatre, reaching the well-positioned Santa Luzia and the adjacent Miradouro Santa Luzia. From there, we had breathtaking views of the river Tejo (Tagus). At the entrance, the statue of Afonso Henrique greeted visitors. In this castle, the Portuguese defeated the Moors, who had lived here in the medieval period, providing a secure and safe rendezvous.

Tile Museum

BELEM TOWER (TORRE DE BELEM)

In 1497, Vasco Da Gama set sail to India from this tower with a small cargo of pepper, which he could sell for sixty times its value. Over the centuries, the River Tejo has receded, but Belem Tower stands like a rock, guarding the entrance to the port.

Porto

On the way back from Belem Tower, we visited the Museu de Arte Antiga, which is the only national gallery in Portugal and is managed by the Gulbenkian Foundation.

PORTO

Known as the capital of the North in Portugal, Porto is unpretentious, inward-looking, and unashamedly commercial. We felt this when Ajita tried to buy a sketch from a street-side artist who refused to budge on the price he had quoted. The city's greatest sights include four bridges across the Douro River, two of which were built in the nineteenth century, and two more modern ones. Porto is a city of undulating terrain, so one needs to be cautious while walking.

We took the semi-bullet train from Santa Apolonia to travel to Porto, which took us three hours. Upon arrival, a Bolt taxi booked by Krishna took us to our hotel, Yotel, located in the midtown area within half an hour. Since the check-in time was at 3 PM, we left our luggage with the concierge staff.

Following the advice of a local, we chose to have lunch at a reasonably good and inexpensive open-air restaurant. We enjoyed Lubiya/rice stew, bread soup, and finished with a sweet dish, Nata, for only Euros 20.

After lunch, we set off on foot towards the Douro River, walking through undulating narrow alleys. As we approached the riverfront, the tourist crowd began to swell. We happened to be in Porto on June 22nd, just before the San Joan festival, a music festival taking place on June 23rd. In the evening, there was music all over the riverfront. People were buying plastic hammers, which they softly used to tap passersby, an age-old customary practice. We observed preparations for the San Joan festivities taking place at various locations.

Here, we visited the Igreja da Trinidade Church. We walked through Aliados Avenida, where we saw the Metro station. The expansion of the underground metro was in full swing, and traffic swirls were visible.

Porto wine is famous, and the older the wine, the better it is, with prices to match. At 9 PM, during sunset, we decided to have our supper, enjoying red wine and chicken wings.

On June 23rd, the celebrations were set to start in the evening, but we couldn't witness them as our train to Lisbon was in the evening. However, we found that our 5:35 PM train was canceled due to a wildcat strike by a section of railway employees. We had to board an unscheduled train to Lisbon. As tourists, we received a warm reception from the regular passengers who accommodated us, understanding the difficulties caused by the strike.

SINTRA

Pena Palace

Sintra was the summer residence of the Kings of Portugal and the Moorish Lords of Lisbon. An old Spanish proverb states, "To see the world and leave out Sintra is to go blind about." Lord Byron stayed here in 1809 and wrote a poem, proclaiming that this place was perhaps the most delightful in every aspect, containing beauties of every description, both natural and artificial. We visited the Pena Palace, perched on the hilltop and uniquely designed by a novice German architect, built in different levels. Walt Disney followed the same unique pattern of this palace in Disneyland. This palace is also surrounded by a beautiful forest consisting of huge tall trees.

We traveled to Sintra by a surface train from Rossio Central Rail Station in Lisbon, reaching there in an hour's time. On arrival, we found ourselves in a tiny fairytale city surrounded by beautiful houses and trees.

THE ALGARVE

With its long sandy beaches and picturesque rugged rocky coves, the Algarve attracts tourists from all over the world. This tourist spot is popular for its exotic natural features, and we found that most of the youngsters, predominantly young Europeans, visit this place on the Atlantic coast for water sports and sunbathing on the beaches. We reached Albufeira, a resort town in Algarve, by an overland bus from Lisbon in three hours.

We set off on a catamaran cruise, which was booked in advance, with a very vibrant group of young tourists, and we cruised on the Atlantic Ocean for three hours. The youngsters were eagerly looking for dolphins, and some of them jumped into the ocean for swimming, while everyone was enjoying themselves to their hearts' content. We enjoyed the vision of the beaches through our binoculars. We returned to Lisbon the same day by an evening bus.

Our fourteen-day trip to Portugal concluded, leaving us with great memories.

www.ingramcontent.com/pod-product-compliance
Lightning Source LLC
LaVergne TN
LVHW061555070526
838199LV00077B/7058